Island Chaplain,

Tristan da Cunha 1975 - 1978

Edmund Digby Buxton

Foreword by
Allan Crawford, FRGS

Published by
George Mann Publications
Easton, Winchester,
Hampshire SO21 1ES
01962 779944

Copyright © E D Buxton 2001
Copyright © George Mann Publications 2001

All rights reserved.
No part of this publication may
be reproduced, stored in a retrieval
system, or transmitted in any form or
by any means, electronic, mechanical,
photocopying, recording or otherwise,
without the prior permission
of the copyright holders.

A CIP catalogue record for this book
is available from the British Library

ISBN 0-95-244247-7

George Mann Publications

Contents

Foreword 5

Preface 7

Remote Arrival – 1975 – Brittanic Outpost 11

Linger – 1976 – Longer 23

Tethered – 1977 – To Tristan 59

Last – 1978 – Lap 75

Tristan Prayers 91

Acknowledgements
Schoolmaster Nigel Humphries and I both took many photographs on Tristan, and in this book I cannot remember who took which, probably mostly his: apologies. *EDB*

Other books by the Edmund Buxton:
Then and Now
Making Prayers
Prayer + Plus

Foreword

When at the age of 88 I was invited to write a foreword, I realised that the author was in his 93rd year! This book records his adventures as incumbent of the loneliest Anglican parish in the world.

Edmund and Katharine early abandoned a life of retirement in Hampshire for a small village of less than 300 population in the Roaring Forties in the South Atlantic Ocean.

However, earlier life and ministry were not without dramatic incidents. In 1939 Edmund became Vicar of his first parish, which was in South East London. In 1940 the parish church there was totally destroyed by a German bomb, and their Vicarage was badly damaged. They were grateful to be offered shared accommodation in a local doctor's house.

After the war Edmund was Vicar of Wembley for ten years, and he and Katharine were also fully occupied with the upbringing of their family of two boys and two girls.

Then a move to Somerset and the parish of Milborne Port, together with a very small parish of Goathill, which perhaps helped to condition him for the forthcoming call out of retirement and at the age of 67 to risk adventure to Tristan da Cunha.

I have for a long time been in frequent communication with the islanders by visits and by correspondence. I know that the Buxtons were gladly welcomed after a gap without a Chaplain; and were respected and loved by the islanders during their three years there.

I wish Edmund well with this book.

Allan Crawford

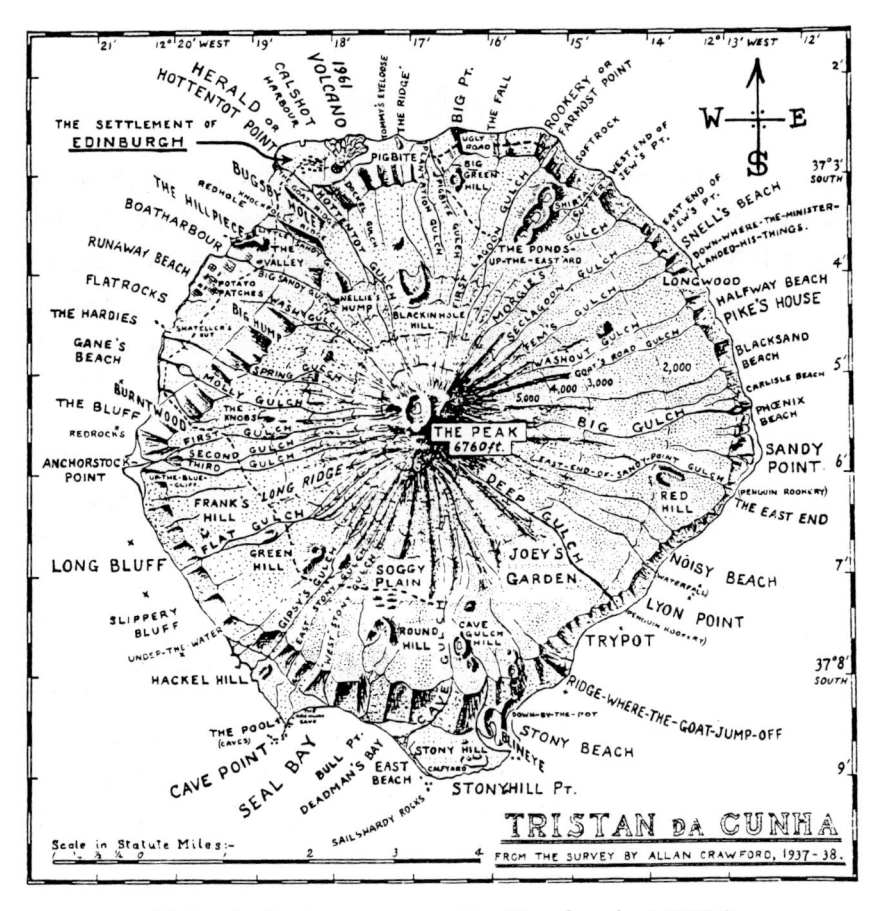

Tristan da Cunha as surveyed by Allan Crawford 1937-8

Preface

It's a mountain in the sea. And it is part of the mid-Atlantic ridge, which includes the Azores, St Helena, Tristan da Cunha, Gough Island. It is about five thousand miles from England and in the middle of the South Atlantic Ocean, midway between South Africa and South America, and two thousands miles from the Falkland Islands. It is the same latitude as Cape Town. Its mountain peak rises to 6760 ft.

This island mountain is roughly circular in shape, and approximately eight miles in diameter, and twenty-four miles in circumference. Situated in the southern hemisphere the seasons are the reverse of ours in Europe; but there are no extremes in temperature, and the rainfall is high. Being in the range of the 'Roaring Forties' it is often subject to very stormy weather.

Tristan da Cunha was discovered in 1506 by a Portuguese navigator and named after him, but it remained uninhabited. There are several smaller islands in the vicinity, notably islands Nightingale and Inaccessible.

In 1816 a British contingent occupied Tristan to prevent any French attempt to rescue Napoleon imprisoned on St Helena. Corporal William Glass of the Royal Artillery and from Kelso in Scotland was in this garrison; and when the object of the exercise was over, he chose to stay on there. He got his wife out and they had a large family. He is regarded with respect and pride as the founder of the island community.

In those early years the tiny population gradually increased with some landing from passing ships, and some ending up there from shipwreck. Six adventurous women were brought from St Helena, when there was a surplus of lonely menfolk on Tristan. The small population includes several original nationalities, but with now only seven surnames between them: Glass, Green, Hagan, Lavarello, Repetto, Rogers, Swain; and all gladly and proudly accept British nationality. Among themselves they are generally known by their first name, or perhaps a nickname.

In 1961 after some strange and sinister warnings, a new volcano erupted close to the settlement. Immediate escape was possible by all the community moving away to the potato patches and their huts there; and the next day two fishing trawlers took them to the greater safety of Nightingale island. But the volcano became so threatening that complete evacuation was an urgent necessity. First to Cape Town; and then accommodation was arranged for them at Fawley and Calshot on Southampton Water.

They found the English winter climate very unacceptable; and after two years it was decided that Tristan was safe for most of them to return, which was their desire and decision. The lava from the 1961 volcano had damaged only one of the island houses, but it had destroyed the fish factory, and two useful landing beaches. It left its grim grey deposit right across the plateau to the east of the settlement, and with now a well trodden track across it.

The trawlers attached to the fishing industry and export are very much part of the island scene and work; and also a link with the outside world by sea with Cape Town, bring and taking mail, and also supplies for the island canteen, etc. and also occasional passengers. Philately has also been a source of income for the island with its stamps and keen collectors around the world.

The island population also included expatriates from overseas, who come and go, some with wives and children. From Britain they are appointed to take responsibility in various departments of island life, such as administration, education, medical, radios and post, farming, and as in my case, a priest for the church. Some visitors come for scientific or research reasons. In the community we were referred to as expats.

In 1974 my wife and I had retired to Hampshire, but the next year this exciting opportunity of travel and adventure and service cropped up – a priest for Tristan da Cunha. I was 67, but I offered, and took the chance. I kept a diary, and this book tells the story of our life there. The frequent use of the letter K refers to my wife Katharine.

Stanley Trees M.V.O., O.B.E. was the Administrator during our 3 years there.

I am so grateful to Allan Crawford for his Foreword and encouragement; and also for his own book on the island as a useful source of information.

Edmund Buxton
10 Pound Hill
Alresford
Hampshire SO24 9BW
England

'The mountain in the sea'

Remote Arrival – 1975 – Brittanic Outpost

October 19, 1975

A barge came out from the harbour to take us off the *RSA*. We were thankful for help up the harbour wall before setting our feet firmly on this 'loneliest island'; and enjoying the warm welcome that awaited us. It had been a lengthy voyage out from Cape Town leaving on October 2 on the *RSA*. We had on board a team of young men from South Africa to replace those on the Met Station on Gough Island. Owing to rough weather we had to anchor there for several days before it was possible to deal with the exchange of men and supplies. On our return trip three years later with no stop at Gough it took only six days from Tristan da Cunha to Cape Town, with strong westerly winds in our favour.

The outward sea voyage was an interesting experience. The German-born captain used to have us up to his cabin to teach us chess. He thought it might be useful to occupy us on perhaps some rather long and empty evenings in our life on the island.

The settlement called Edinburgh is on the north side of the island and about one hundred feet up from the harbour. It is situated on a ledge or plateau at the bottom of the mountain, and this extends east and west about six miles long, and is never more than half a mile wide.

The island community live in this settlement of about one hundred houses, long, low and close together, and making up together with expatriates a population of about three hundred. On the face of it it looked like a possible job for an elderly retired priest!

There are of course other buildings such as the fish factory, the church, the school, the hospital, post office and radio shack and administration buildings. The chaplain's house is a nice bungalow above the harbour and looking out to sea. This makes for a site and situation such as we have not experienced before, so that will be new and exciting for us.

Island Harbour

29.11.75

Our outlook is usually a wide expanse of empty ocean, but today a small single-masted yacht appeared. This seems to be an event and an excuse important enough to stop all work at the school, and to bring teachers and children out to a vantage point to have a look. It doesn't happen often.

We scrambled up Hottentot Gulch to the large white stone, a good wide view point, and where we enjoyed the company of a 'starchy' (Tristan thrush), very friendly as it hopped around us.

3.12.75
A ship will be leaving for Cape Town and this is posting day. We have seventy-six letters ready. We hope they will reach their destination, because they say Tristan stamps are a temptation!

5.12.75
Pastoral work here can obviously be very personal. A man has been very ill in hospital and I have been several times to see him. This evening I was at his bedside with some of his family. At 2.30 a.m. I was called out again, as he had died, and they expected prayers before he was laid out.

As with this funeral, so with a wedding or baptism, all such are very much community events, and this means that we can penetrate and participate more fully in the life of the people.

6.12.75
Still struggling over names – in fact it is almost getting worse. It's so unfair! All of them know a newcomer at once, because you are the exception and a rather rare event. A new face so conspicuous and with of course a new name. But nothing like as quick and easy the other way round; and there can be that embarrassing look of surprise, "you don't know me yet?"

We walked up to Hillpiece and sat there to enjoy the splendid views, both back to the settlement, and in the other direction out to the potato patches, and across the sea out to Inaccessible Island.

7.12.75
Sunday after church is a very social time for getting together in each other's houses. I had to see Lars Repetto, the Lay Reader, about something, and of course I was asked in. There were about a dozen people there, and I knew them all by name. So I am making progress!

The settlement called Edinburgh

9.12.75
To the school for prayers and teaching. Then I went to the treasurer's department to pay in the church collection money. I also discussed plans for Christmas with the Administrator.

This afternoon I went out in the factory barge to fish from off the trawler *Melodie* with our young doctor. We caught quite a lot of 'five-fingers' fish.

A two-masted yacht arrived from California and anchored off the island.

12.12.75
At the early Communion Service in the church there was a curious noise above our heads. It turned out to be ducks which had easily popped up onto the church roof from the high bank alongside. And this afternoon at the end of term service for the school children a dog kept coming into the church – again diversion and distraction!

14.12.75
I invited six families who had had a baby baptised by the Lay Reader since the last Chaplain left the island. He hinted that they might feel that a 'finishing touch' from the new Chaplain might be appropriate and acceptable. So we had words of welcome, prayer and blessing for those who had been baptised. And I asked for each child to be brought up by the mother. I gave her a card and laid my hand in blessing on the child's head.

I am making Saturday a day off as much as possible. I get on with the preparation for Sunday early in the week, and Saturday comes as a break and a breather to blow away the cobwebs, and to clear the mind for Sunday and worship.

15.12.75

The doctor and his wife are joining in a meat trip to Stoney Beach. We had watched the factory barge filled to capacity with about a dozen persons, and towing two dinghies setting off round the island. And at the end of the day they returned with six cattle carcasses cut up, and to be off-loaded.

The Administrator was not at all pleased. An Island Council meeting had been arranged for today and several members had gone off on that expedition. We could not muster a quorum. It looks as if the weather is the dictator on this island, and perhaps the factory is its commissar?

19.12.75

We are trying to visit every house; and we have two teenage girls as helpful guides. We offer a copy of St Luke's gospel as a small Christmas gift. Visiting takes time, as it should; but conversation is apt to slacken off after a bit. There is not a great variety of subjects to talk about – the weather and the sea, the fishing and the factory, the potatoes... But you must not seem to hurry away. A time of silence doesn't matter at all. To be together is the important thing. If I get up to go, "You'se in a hurry, Father!"

I called this evening on the Factory Manager to offer my services to his fishing vessels over the Christmas season, but he tells me that they will be away off Gough Island.

We have a letter ready for the post to be shared by two families with whom we have close links.

> *Dear Hargreaves and Hunts,*
> *We've been here nearly six weeks, so we have begun to get our bearings. It has been quite a stiff job of adjustment to a full-time commitment again, after having tasted the sweets of*

retirement; but God called us, and we asked for it!

In this small close-knit community names and family relationships have been rather confusing, and hard but urgent to sort out. Everyone is known by his or her first name. They are all so friendly and welcome us into their homes. Conversation is apt to dry up – after all what is there to talk about except the family and the weather and the fishing and the potatoes!

We are getting used to their sometimes quaint way of speaking. A man said to me, "You know my sister Haggernees" with such assurance that I meekly nodded. Fortunately it quickly dawned on me that he was referring to Agnes, who comes in to us once a week to help in the house.

Our main service on Sunday is the 8 a.m. Eucharist with hymns and sermon. At 10.30 a.m. there is a Children's Service, and it is a tricky exercise trying to cope with ages from a few weeks or months to 14 years old. Evensong with sermon is at 6 p.m.

We have long free evenings and plenty of time for reading. Our island library has quite a wide choice of books, which gives us a chance of catching up on some of the English classics, And I have launched into Tolkien's 'Lord of the Rings', which I am enjoying. Partly because it's a bit of a 'hobbit' situation here with long low houses tucked into the ground, and with their stable doors, the top half nearly always open.

Gardens are getting nice and colourful with summer here now. Vegetables grow well in the alluvial soil and protected from the strong winds by huge plants of flax, which can grow up to ten feet high. We have picked our first radishes.

Out to sea are albatross, skuas and terns to be seen, and walking along the shore we have spotted rockhopper penguins. We are told that they will soon invade the settlement, as they

Lava from the 1961 volcano and the settlement beyond it

come up every summer to moult. We shall welcome them!
The whole extent of the shelf or plateau about 100 feet above the sea is about six or seven miles, so we do have plenty of scope for walking. And over against us rising steeply 2000ft is the mountain base. Above that it rises up to the peak at nearly 7,000ft with its extinct volcanic crater. The islanders always talk about going east or west, and that is the way that the shelf lies as it faces north.

So we are settling in happily. The expatriates here are a first-rate lot, a young doctor and his wife, a young Scot agricultural officer, a keen Christian schoolmaster and his wife and three children, a PWD man and his wife, and a 'sparker' to deal with radio and post. Next door to us is the Administrator and his wife, and he obviously has the welfare of the community as his chief concern.

22.12.75
I was sworn in as a member of the Island Council, and also elected as its Vice President. I appreciate the honour, but I can only hope that the President does not go sick or is called away – both for my sake and for that of the island!

CHRISTMAS 1975
For the midnight service the church began to fill by 10 p.m. I took in our cassette player, and we had some parts of Handel's Messiah, while they waited. The church looked lovely with its new carpet, the crib and the flowers; and there was new tiling on the vestry floor. We had over a hundred communicants, and also a good attendance at the Children's Service in the morning.

With the closing of the factory and with no fishing, the community are like a people liberated, to go their own way and to do their own thing. In their houses and homes they are painting and papering walls, repairing floors and ceilings; and always of course there are the patches and the potatoes.

There are expeditions to Stoney Beach and to the Cave and Sandy Point for cattle and sheep. The sheep are brought back alive; and then killed beside their houses, skinned and cut up. The meat is taken to the public freezer and stored in the family locker there. They have been so kind to us, bringing gifts of meat, potatoes and eggs.

26.12.75
We scrambled up to the 250 ft top of the new volcano of the 1961 eruption. A small boy came up behind us. He had been told that Father Christmas lived up there. When he came down they asked him, "Well, did you see Father Christmas?" "No," he replied, "but I saw Father Buxton."

On the corner of the path above our house appeared a rockhopper penguin. We gently coaxed it through our gate, hoping it might stay a while, but it soon disappeared in the thick of the flax.

Whole families and households "stay" with each other during the Christmas holidays, sharing together in the daylight hours, but sleeping still in their own homes.

28.12.75
We had the chance to attempt to climb the 2000ft base of the mountain with Herbert Glass as our very competent companion and guide. It was not too difficult, but I was thankful for the firm grip of a strong hand in one or two places. Unfortunately the weather deteriorated; and we got up only into mist and cloud, and had no view of the peak.

We came down a different way, slipping and sliding on loose scree. We were met at the bottom by Barbara and Monica who had come along with coffee and cake to cheer and to refresh us. What a kind thought!

30.12.75
New Year's Eve and a frivolous entertainment. Some of the young men dressed up so as to conceal their identity completely, including queer head-dress and mask; and allowing no indication or recognition by tone of voice. They then set about seeming to threaten or harass young ladies in the vicinity, which could be rather frightening and alarming. And she would have no idea as to who it might be! When time is up and the romp over, the rogues and ruffians remove their disguise and reveal their identity with a lot of laughter to excuse apology!

We have added a small flower bed in front of the house, and transported some pansies which had come on well on our vegetable plot; and they make a colourful patch.

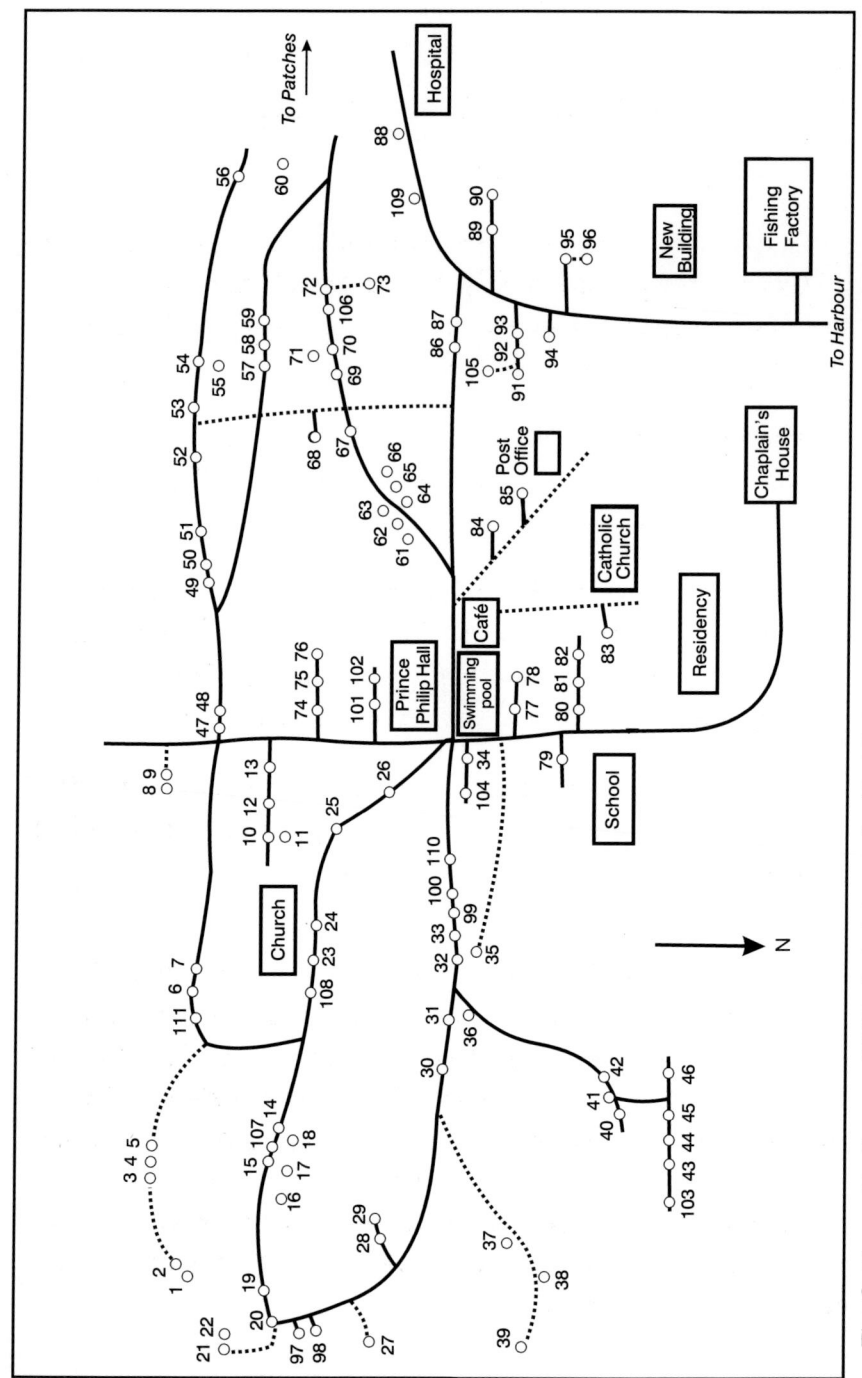

The Settlement in the year 2000. A sketch map by 'Pat' Paterson who came out to Tristan as an expat 'Sparker' (radio and post), while we were there. He married an islander, Susan Green. They have two daughters and now live in England.

Linger – 1976 – Longer

3.1.76
The *Melodie* has been here all day at anchor, for fish to be taken off for processing in the factory. The packaged crayfish are then taken back on board, together with our mail, for Cape Town; and then exported to USA and to Japan.

Julian came in with a gift of potatoes from his parents. He was delighted with my big book of Edward Wilson's bird sketches, and he asked to borrow it.

Potatoes still pour in. Marian brought some, and long delayed her departure. There is a timeless feature of life here. Can you imagine teenagers in England ringing the Vicarage bell, and popping in from time to time for a leisurely visit?

This morning at Communion a collie dog came into the church and right up to me in the sanctuary just as I turned to the people to read the comfortable words, "Come unto me..."

11.1.76
A full Sunday. At 8 a.m. Holy Communion I gave out the first hymn... but no sound, no organist. K came to the rescue and took over; but still no sound from the congregation. Tune unknown, so I changed the hymn. In the course of my sermon I ventured to suggest something like an anti-litter campaign. Later Nigel came to see me, and gently and kindly informed me that there was resentment over my hints about alcohol and litter. I take note and accept the rebuke; but I am sure that there must always be a link between religion and life.

At the Children's Service we had Alison Swain's baptism; and afterwards it was round to their house to celebrate.

In a fancy dress party after Christmas I went as a dustbin, with an old grey carpet round my middle, and with bare legs. With two notices attached — KEEP TRISTAN TIDY on my front, and LEAVE NO LITTER on my back, I hoped for a smile to take away resentment, and perhaps acceptance of challenge to change.

15.1.76
The *Hilary* arrived early and anchored, and our hopes ran high! We had seen the tractor with trailer taking the mail bags up to the Post Office, then patient waiting.

At last, at midday, a call at our door with our mailbag. Eagerly we took it, and emptied the contents on the floor. There were well over one hundred letters, packages and parcels.

Familiar writing first catches the eye; then the guessed at; and after that the unknown add to the excitement. And what a variety of reactions as you read. But as with a tasty dish, it is possible to overindulge; and with this mass of mail there comes a sense of surfeit. You just cannot take any more. You have to stop, and do something else. Go out and get some fresh air. Come back and start again, and then there are still some unopened. And so many to read again!

Yes, the arrival of mail is very definitely an important feature of life on Tristan! Even as it takes you right away from it.

18.1.76
A double-masted yacht came into view from the west. There was a Frenchman on board. He anchored offshore all day to take in fresh water and vegetables. About 5 p.m. he was running up his sails, and before long his boat was a tiny speck on the horizon –

what freedom, what independence, what economy of fuel! And adventure too!

We called on Churchwarden Douglas and found him cutting Carol's hair. We were invited in and with four others watched the amateur performance.

Chaplain's House

21.1.76
Queen's Day and it was celebrated with a reception at the Residency. Later there were fun and games outside; and then a dance in the hall in the evening.

We had our first Mother's Union service and meeting with about two dozen members. They came round to tea with us afterwards.

The Church Commissioners have written about pension payments, asking me to write quarterly as evidence that I am still alive. Do they think that I am rather old to have taken on this job? Or do they have grave doubts about the volcano? I have written telling them that they cannot rely on regular postings from here; and that anyhow they would quickly be aware, if I became a victim of a volcanic eruption!

25.1.76
Sunday and we celebrate St Paul's conversion, a very exciting event and dramatic. Also of very great importance in the history of our Christian faith. Pentecost and Paul's conversion, two big events that opened gates into a wider world.

26.1.76
Nightingale at last! They say it has been the longest wait for many years. Eight long-boats to go and all was bustle and hustle in the harbour; and then with sails up they were out and away westward. It was a lovely sight.

The long-boats* are made on the island by skilful construction and from long experience; and for sure the sea is very much part of the life of the island. Nightingale island, twenty-five miles away across the sea to the south west, is a valuable asset; and also an occasional way of escape from the confines of the settlement life.

We were taken over the fish factory and saw the women at work, processing and packing the crayfish tails. We were also shown the generating plant making electricity for the entire settlement.

* *We have an exact model of a Tristan longboat skilfully made by Gordon Glass. He lost an arm in an accident on the island, so he only had one hand for modelling. He stayed in Fawley with his wife Susan, and we were with them when they celebrated the 70th anniversary of their wedding.*

Longboat
photograph by Nigel Humphries

30.1.76

Boats back from Nightingale on a lovely day of blue sky and white clouds and with a sufficient fresh breeze. And a whole holiday for the school – any excuse will do! But this time there is good reason: the women are busy cooking and preparing for those returning.

There was a general movement to get a good view out to sea. And there were the long boats dotted about on the water in colourful array. They compete as to be the first to make the harbour. We went back and watched the off-loading; and then the tractor hauling the boats back up to their base beside the school.

We are told of a schoolmaster who came out from England. He left after only a few months, because he was afraid the mountain was going to fall on him. I must admit that the mighty bastion of the base does sometimes appear a bit sinister and almost threatening; but I don't think that will frighten us away!

1.2.76
Tomorrow's festival is linked with our Patron Saint. What to call it? Presentation? Purification? Candlemas? Or perhaps, and why not, Old Folk's Festival – recalling Simeon and Anna in Luke 2?

Reading Lamb's Essays and Letters, I am intrigued by his reaction to his own retirement in 1825, and by his sense of freedom, deliverance, emancipation! He writes, "I came home FOR EVER on Tuesday in last week. The incomprehensibleness of my condition overwhelmed me! It was like passing from time into eternity..." To another he wrote, "My weather-glass stands at a degree or two above CONTENT."

My experience and my weather-glass in 1974 was several degrees below 'Content', and my weather 'unsettled'.

3.2.76
Early this morning the *Tristania* arrived bringing the new doctor and his wife. And again a bag of mail was brought to our door, and our day was lush with letters. I also went out on the factory barge and fished off the *Tristania*. I enjoyed a cup of coffee and a talk with the Captain.

Charlie came round this evening bringing himself and a fine home-grown cabbage as a gift. He lingered over a can of beer and leisurely conversation, mostly vegetarian.

6.2.76
We had the new doctor and his wife to lunch. This evening there was a farewell dance for the departing doctor and his wife. It was

fun after I had got over my hesitation, and had ventured to ask one of the opposite sex to risk it. We shall miss Keith and Alison. In a short time they have become very much a part of island life, not to mention their scatter-brained dog, Jethro.

We have added about eighty letters to the outgoing mail.

10.2.76
If my first impression was that of shyness and reserve among the children, it has been changed by their behaviour in school. And lively they can be in church too. This morning I got a pew full of children to act the healed lepers, and to go on their way to report to the priest; and one of them to turn back and to throw herself at my feet, giving thanks for healing. That did cause some excitement.

K had rather a fluid situation in her class at school with frequent exits to the loo. When one small boy asked for a second time to be excused, she thought there should be a limit. However, Robin insisted, "Please, Miss, I done bust for wee." Too much for K, and he slipped through her fingers.

13.2.76
Because so much depends upon the weather, there is always a clear indication early in the morning if it is to be a fishing day. A metal cylinder is struck loud and clear several times. So it was today, but some in their long boats decided it was to be Nightingale for them, and there were signs of activity in the harbour. I said to K, "Where is the wind to take them to Nightingale?" Presently we heard it was off; but it was too late to make it a fishing day.

15.2.76

Headmaster Nigel is off sick; and K and I are helping to fill the gap. Beverley's very loud voice in my class called for a comment from Rita, "Father, do you know what we call her?" "No," I said, "What?" "Loud hailer," she answered. "Very apt," I said. And for the rest of that period Beverley made no more noise than a loud mouse.

21.2.76

In our usual Saturday walk we climbed Hillpiece to get a good view of the returning long boats from Nightingdale. Presently small patches of colour, and the sails were to be seen rounding the bluff very slowing, as the wind was so light.

We then walked to the "tree" – the one and only evergreen fir tree by the Walsh gulch. We do miss trees here.

A sudden downpour during the service on Sunday made a lot of noise on the metal roof of the church, and took everybody by surprise. The service ended and nobody moved – they had come to church quite unprepared, and now had to wait until the storm subsided. Lars said he had never known the congregation thus defeated, cabined and confined!

24.2.76

At the Church Council we discussed plans for Lent and Holy Week; and also the possibility of evening Communion, especially for those at work during the day. And there was the question whether to try to use the new South African Liturgy 1975?

26.2.76

We called on Auntie Martha Rogers just as her girls (as she calls her large middle-aged friendly helpers) were tidying up, after spending the day there carding and spinning wool.

We had a cable from the Archbishop of Cape Town telling us that Bishop Leslie Stradling will be coming out here in October 1977 for a Confirmation. Very good news and a target date; but also allowing time for preparation.

1.3.76
My birthday at 68 – the age my father died. I hope I don't – not out here anyhow. We kept it quiet, because I do not want the publicity and celebration, which is the order of the day for birthdays here.

We had an old English breakfast with fried eggs on toast and mushrooms, which I had picked locally. For lunch we had tasty mutton rissoles and corn on the cob with melted butter (which I had first eaten in New York in 1930!); and then one of K's perfect steam puddings. Very tasty celebration, if rather aloof.

6.3.76
Weather today rather as we had visualised it before we came – boisterous with wind and rain, and the mountain over against us almost invisible, clouded and shrouded to the foot of the base.

'Cup o' Tea Tristan' – around houses this afternoon I had a cup at George and Liza; then another cup with Kate; then another with Ken and Emily, where I asked Jimmy to be reserve server in church; then another with dear Maud looking after her gorgeous grandchildren, Noelene and Desirée... then a dash for home.

10.3.76
We were hoping to complete our round of first visits to each house this week; but it is difficult always to catch them at home. They are so busy now at their potato patches, digging our potatoes and bringing them back in sacks, and leaving seed potatoes out there.

There is the occasional fishing day, but only small catches at this time of year. Should there be a closed season to allow stocks to replenish?

15.3.76
Island Council, and I now know the members better. Anti-litter project on the agenda. We had recently picked up twenty tin cans within a stone's throw of the litter bins outside the Prince Philip Hall. I had prepared a report, and we had a useful discussion. Gavin (expat farmer) came to deal with his department – cows, sheep, donkeys, pasture, etc.

We went to the radio shack and talked over the air to the men on Gough Island, who were with us on the *RSA* last October coming out here.

25.3.76
Lady Day and the day of our island Patron Saint, the Blessed Virgin Mary. At Holy Communion a little ladybird appeared on my book, yellow with black spots. Such a joy to behold and so timely too! It is the first I have seen here; and we are rather lacking, it seems, in variety of insect life.

28.3.76
Mothering Sunday. We had prepared seventy cards, and had got the children to fill them in with their own drawings and greetings. We invited mothers to our Children's Service; and the children gave the cards to their mothers there.

We celebrate birthdays at the beginning of the service by singing, "Happy Birthday to You"... This we did for Sharon, aged 11, one of the brightest and best youngsters.

The Chaplain and his wife

3.4.76
Three dinghies made a dash to Sandy Point for apples. They had a hard pull in rough weather; and one in emergency had to row for the nearest beach.

I am reading Bishop John Taylor's 'Go-Between God'. He quotes a discovery of a linguistic expert that sometimes more is relayed from person to person through the pauses and hesitations of speech than through its words. "It takes more time and delicacy to learn the silence of people than to learn its sounds." A lesson for us here – anywhere?

5.4.76
Appling Day is an annual event. Five dinghies left the harbour. We went in the barge, and it took two hours to get to Sandy Point.

From the sea we had some good close-up views of the mountain, fissured and ravined with a succession of great gulches along its side. We didn't have long there. They shook the trees in order to bring back as many apples as possible, but losing a lot in the process.

Agnes was kind enough to be at the harbour on our return with a thermos of tea – such a kind thought; and a habit it seems to be.

6.4.76
Egrets are now often to be seen, sometimes battling against strong winds with their slow wing beats, making it look like a very unequal struggle.

K cut my hair in the garden this afternoon.

12.4.76
I wanted to tidy up the church garden for Easter, and I asked one or two after the Children's Service to come and help. Almost spontaneously we had a gang of enthusiastic young workers – Beverley, Rita, Nigel, Jeremy, Paul, all very keen and busy non-stop. And afterwards they cleared up, with one of them dashing off and getting a wheelbarrow about twice as big as himself.

At an election for the new Island Council the response was – 135 votes out of a possible 199 with Albert Glass still Chief Islander, getting the highest score in votes.

Some men are shirking over the hefty job of making concrete dolosses for the harbour surround. They are finding an easy way of escape by going to the doctor complaining of aches and pains; and they are very pleased to take his advice to ease off!

16.4.76
Good Friday, and a full church before we started at midday for the Three Hours devotion. I divided it into three sections, with hymns and periods of silence too.

18.4.76
EASTER on Tristan
Out and up to the church at 6.30 a.m. Clear dawn just breaking, but several bright stars still shining. The church was dark, but rapidly filling. I lit the Paschal candle. Before the service began we listened on a cassette to resurrection music from the Messiah as recorded in Guildford Cathedral.

At Evensong I was rather tired, but the sight of old Liza singing the Magnificat with wee Wendy in her arms, and with such a happy loving look in her eyes, must have brought a smile upon the face of Mary above.

The Potato Patches
photograph by Philippe Godard

TIMETABLE ON TRISTAN

Somebody's running on Tristan
What's all the hurry about?
Well –
Longboats are leaping
And Nightingale's calling –   (1)
Patches are popping
With potatoes for digging –

But
Dangling 'dong' disturbing dawn
Has sounded 'fishing today' …
And the factory is full
Of lobsters processing   (2)
Tristan's salt-water gold –

Knives, axes, guns
The weapons are ready
From Stoney Beach pasture   (3)
There is meat for the table –

The apples are ripening
So on the agenda
Sandy Point also must go –   (4)

Cattle are moo-ing
Can't wait to be milked
And Gavin says, Change fence today – (5)

There's building and making
Improvements, enlargements –
You won't know our house
When this job is done –   (6)

Needles are clicking
And wool is unwinding
Don't leave it behind
But knit as you go.   (7)

The canteen is open
But soon it is closing
And food and refreshment
Must be provided –
Each birthday's a date   (8)
To keep and celebrate.

And now
Quick! To the harbour
We must welcome our menfolk
The boats are in sight!   (9)

No wonder you sometimes sit still
Silent and still
Long time sometimes
Sit still
And anyhow
night must fall …

And day-star arise
The Old Man is calling a Council   (10)
But that like all else will depend
On the wind and the wave
The two hands of the clock
That will always determine
Time table and program
On Tristan.

(1) Nightingale Island about 25 miles to the west. Islanders sail there in their longboats for birds, eggs, fat, guano.
(2) The 'dong' is an old metal cylinder struck early in the morning when the weather is suitable for fishing.
(3) A pasture on the south side of the island with a herd of cattle.
(4) Sandy Point on the east side with apple trees.
(5) Gavin Jack was Agricultural Officer. Fences are sections of pasture land fenced off.
(6) Islanders are constantly making alterations, improvements, decoration to their houses, especially before Christmas, or additions for a young married couple.
(7) Constant use of local wool.
(8) Canteen is the island store or shop.
(9) With food and drink – as they always do.
(10) The Administrator is sometimes called the Old Man and he presides over the Island Council.

2.5.76

We had used the new 1975 Liturgy of the Church of the Province of South Africa for the first time, and it seemed to be fairly acceptable. One or two said they liked something about its freshness. But it had nothing to do with a dog running along the outside metal top of the church, just as I began to say the prayer, "The Lord is here" (bang, bang overhead), "Lift up your hearts" (thump, thump). Canine accompaniment – liturgical extravaganza!

In England we would be happy welcoming a most lovely colourful month of the year full of new growth and colour; but here now we are moving into winter.

6.5.76

Long boats returned late from Nightingale owing to delayed start back, and only a light wind. One boat got a rent in its canvas as they were loading up.

I joined the boat trip to the caves. Five young heifers had to be tied up and loaded on, and then later to be liberated onto the distant pasture. When we got there the rather wild cattle were chased by the men with their rifles and shot. They were immediately skinned and cut up. Then the pieces were carried to the boats for taking back: a rather gruesome and bloody exercise.

Gavin has been worried about the number of donkeys. There are about three dozen consuming precious pasture, and only six or seven are really needed.

8.5.76
Saturday and preparing the church for Harvest Festival, with some helpful girls making a colourful display. There was a full church on Sunday for the Thanksgiving. We contributed carrots, tomatoes and beetroots from our garden.

Acting on a suggestion of the Church Council I asked the congregation to stay at the end of the service, hoping then and there to deal with the business of the Annual Church Meeting with nominations, etc. But it didn't work. There was almost total lack of any audible response to any request from me for nominations. In such an open setting or public occasion they are too shy and reserved to express a personal opinion. It is the result of being such a small close-knit community. It certainly made for the shortest Annual Parochial Church Meeting I have ever known!

Such hesitation and shyness was not at all evident in the Children's Service later. I was playing a calypso version of the Lord's Prayer with a twanging guitar accompaniment on a cassette. Two small boys quite spontaneously popped out of their pew, joined hands, and started to dance to it together, causing much amusement. I was delighted and said so.

19.5.76

Fishing day, but very few crayfish. Quite a large catch of other fish. Kind gifts later came to our door brought by children, which adds charm to the gifts.

A donkey got its head through a large cardboard carton which remained stuck round its neck. It was a comical sight, but very unhappy for the bothered and perplexed creature. It made it so restless that it was hard to remove the offending object, but I did manage to do so.

21.5.76

A day of hot sun and temperature well over 80°, and we are now well into winter.

A German cargo ship of about 10,000 tons dropped mail for us to post to Cape Town on one of our trawlers. A welcome link with the outside world after weeks of an ocean full of emptiness!

23.5.76

Sunday and the children at 10.30 service were good and attentive; but attendance and behaviour are as variable and unpredictable as is the weather on Tristan!

Peter took me out fishing in a dinghy. We caught a lot in an hour, and I could see our volcano peak for the first time. But my tummy put a limit to it and I succumbed to mal de mer. Peter told me of two remedies – scoop up and drink a mouthful of sea water, or tie a potato round your neck!

27.5.76

Mail came on the *Tristania*. We had over two hundred items; but it is fifteen weeks since the last mail, so there has been a big gap accounting for that hefty score.

When the ship left five days later some expatriates left the island on leave, including the Humphries family. They will be missed especially in school and church. We are happy to look after their very handsome border collie Merlin, while they are away.

26.5.76
At the Education Committee the Administrator spoke of getting the older children further on than at present, and perhaps of getting another qualified teacher out from the UK. He also spoke of the possibility of school leavers getting further training elsewhere in order to come back to the island, and perhaps be able to take over a department here, replacing an expat.

Julian, a bright and lively boy, has left school. There was hope that he might go away for further training, and then perhaps take some special responsibility back on the island.

> ISLAND COUNCIL: Anti-Litter Campaign
> Tristan da Cunha Local Radio Broadcast
> Sunday evening, 27 June 1976
>
> *Last February the Island Council launched, or perhaps I should say renewed, the Keep Tristan Tidy campaign. At the last and recent meeting of the Council it was suggested that another broadcast on the local radio might help, and the Administrator has asked me to do this tonight.*
>
> *I think most of us would agree that we want to keep our homes and houses clean and tidy. How far ought we to do the same thing outside our home? As far as our gardens and immediate surroundings? Surely yes. But no further? Does it matter?*
>
> *I preached about it in church because I think tidiness and*

orderliness are very important for us all and also a part of Christian faith and living according to the Bible. I hope I have always tried, as they say, to "practise what I preach", and so I have been picking up any litter I come across and putting it away in dust bins.

I think the settlement here is looking tidier and cleaner now, and perhaps to that extent the anti-litter campaign has had some effect. But I have a fear that this is largely due to one or two individuals and is not yet accepted by all of us as a good idea and the right thing to do. It will obviously fail if it is no more than the work of an expat who is here today and gone tomorrow. It must be the active, constant and continuing concern of everybody, young and old, with a proper pride and love for this our island home.

2.6.76
In the furious forceful wind, you have to bend almost double to make any progress against it; but walking in its same direction you feel as if any moment you could be whisked off your feet and sent flying!

I had a letter to Tristan's Chaplain from India starting with 'Dear Holy Father' – certainly the highest nomenclature I am ever likely to reach in ecclesiastical elevation and esteem! Positively papist.

Ratting Day is an annual event and a public holiday. The men make up into teams with their dogs to seek and search for rats or mice especially along the stone walls. We took a picnic lunch out to the patches, but there was not any excitement or chase. At the end of the day the team able to show the highest number of tails is the winner. Then there is a dance to celebrate.

He/she was 'tight' last night does not mean 'drunk', I'm glad to say. It is their way of describing a rather bad turn in one of the bronchial or asthmatic sufferers.

12.6.76
The doctor thinks that the wife of an expat may be in need of an urgent operation. But how to get her to Cape Town? There is a Dutch cargo ship willing to change course and call here to pick her up. For three days the sea was too rough to get her on board. Then it moderated and it was possible to take her and her husband. It was a very costly exercise.

We have been wading through copies of *The Times*. They arrive in bulk on a ship from Cape Town. They are dumped first on the Administrator; and he then passes them on to us. It helps to fill in what we have heard on the BBC radio world news service.

A couple of islanders asked for a blessing on their marriage; as they had been married when there was no priest here. I used part of the marriage service with a blessing of the ring. And as they knelt, little Carlene (Stella's daughter by her previous husband Joseph who was drowned) knelt beside them, and I laid my hand upon her head.

A purple iris is flowering outside our bedroom window, and this in mid-winter!

4.7.76
What a shock on returning home after church! Our back door was open, and our home had very obviously suffered an invasion and occupation during our absence.
Chaos in the kitchen and droppings all over the place – a fowl invasion! But no sign of life! Merlin, generally a good watchdog with a loud bark, had failed badly. She was in effect the culprit,

because she must have managed to push the door open and let herself out, and the hens in! Through an open door..

With the dog out of the way and a door ajar, our hens saw their opportunity and took full advantage of it. They had been up on the dresser where they had demolished a pot of apricot jam, bread and butter slices and a packet of margarine. They scorned a bag of their own meal, when a variety of human fare was there available for the pecking.

We wondered why they were not all perched comfortably and contentedly for the night on the backs of chairs or the settee; but no, having had their fill, they had left their visiting cards and returned well-satisfied to their own hen-house. We could only let our imagination play upon the scene, and wish that Beatrix Potter could have pictured and described it!

Two young children came with a kind gift and we asked them in. K read them one or two stories. When she gently suggested that it was time to go home, Judith replied promptly with an emphatic, "No."

The Administrator gave a stern message over the island radio with reference to a theft by three young men, and the fines imposed on them.

15.7.76
There have been two committees on two days, and I am chairman of both. One was called at a couple of hours notice, and there was a full attendance! An advantage of living cheek-by-jowl?

Several people have remarked how well Merlin is looking. She is a lovely creature and has become very attached – except for that Sunday evening leaving an open door!!

22.7.76
At the Administrator's request I have taken over the meteorological readings during the absence of the expat in charge. This means keeping a check on wind and visibility, temperature, barometer, and rainfall; and reporting each day by radio to Gough Island met. station. They tell me to make sure of the wind direction, because it sometimes bounces off the mountain! Visibility test can be measured by how clearly – or if at all – I can see Inaccessible Island.

Quite a chilly SW wind today. I am glad of K's newly knitted red cardigan. We hardly ever have any heating on in the house, and electric current is very expensive.

We were invited by Judy and Ken to Vanessa's first birthday – always a special celebration. We sat down to a well-laden table with meat and potatoes, pumpkin and cabbage; then a variety of sweets including Tristan pudding cooked in a bag with potato mixture, berries, sugar and spice to taste.

30.7.76
Thirty-six years ago we were married... 'To have and to hold, from this day forward; for better, for worse, for richer, for poorer, in sickness and in health...' I think we might have added 'at home, or abroad'.

I picked up a bird with a light grey back and a white chest and broad beak. They call it a night bird, because it flies onto the island by night. I think it nests on the mountain side.

We saw our first whale out to sea through my binoculars as it twisted and turned and dived with its great tail to be seen out of the water.

15.8.76

Another island Patronal Festival – the Blessed Virgin Mary. At our Eucharist this morning I took the line that life with Jesus did not always make it easier or more placid for his Mother; rather the reverse – more demanding and disciplined with challenging situations, interruptions, and also lessons to be learned...

And at the Children's Service we had short readings by some of the girls to help us to form mental pictures of Mary; and then at the end to use it in our home-made prayers with their response "Like Mary" *(see my Tristan Prayers supplement)*.

Old Dick is suffering with much pain in his tummy. The doctor had him into the hospital, and gave him the full works – thin tube up his nose and down inside him, blood drips in the wrist, etc. I don't know how much was really necessary, but when I went to see him I found Dick duly impressed and pleased with himself.

15.8.76

Sunshine and blue sky – at last! After days of grey gloom and dismal damp. The warm sunshine penetrates and pleasantly permeates flesh and bones. I bask in it!

Merlin on heat; and why is it that the least attractive dog is most attracted and persistent towards her? A mongrel here is an awful nuisance. I walked Merlin up to the owner's house closely followed of course, but manage I did to get rid of the pest anyhow for a while. It gave Merlin her exercise free-range, and she took full advantage of it.

The 1961 volcano is 'smocking' as they call it. It does look quite threatening! I suppose it still has fire in its belly.

The Administrator's wife picked some watercress from the

stream and kindly brought some round to us. It made us homesick for our Hampshire watercress beds! There is a never failing stream of fresh water flowing from the base of the mountain. They call it Big Watron.

There is carding and spinning wool in many houses now. Auntie Martha and two others plucking at wool from black and white fleeces to mix and mingle before carding.

7.9.76
Two islanders married and the church was packed, including some expats who otherwise never come. In my address I took the story from John 6 and especially the words, 'Then were they glad to take Jesus into their boat.' Feasting followed almost non-stop, including lunch and supper.

On the radio this evening I told them about the great prison reformer, Elizabeth Fry, and said that she was my great, great, great Aunt!

9.9.76
Mail arrived on *Melodie*. A clear cold morning and the little ship was such a welcome sight making her way across the calm blue sea, with a white wake following.

Copies of *The Times* help us to catch up with world news. I see the Methodist Church has been getting into communication with the Roman Catholics with a view to closer links. Good for them! Bypassing the Church of England which gave them the cold shoulder. Laughter in heaven?

We have despatched 170 letters etc. on the ship leaving.

19.9.76
Early this morning there were thin veils of mist at the top of the base – blue mist, thrush egg blue, and blending with the blue of the sky above.

Our bath has been well used lately in a variety of ways. I gave dog Merlin a bath. Our chicks have turned out to be five cocks and only two hens. We got a man to reduce our cocks to two. After killing three cocks, he plunged them into a bath of hot water before he plucked them.

We also have children bringing us gifts of penguin eggs.

21.9.76
A lovely day and Merlin agreed to a long walk. We passed many island folk on their way to the patches to plant out their potatoes. Some were out in different directions collecting penguin eggs.

Along the way we saw the remains of wee lambs, which had been killed by skuas and picked to the bone. Effects of the recent heavy rains were obvious by the deposits of huge boulders on the track where it crosses two gulches.

Tired by the end of the day, but I am happy after we have cleared away supper and washed up. There is a chess board between us on the table, and the pieces are in place ready for encounter and contest. Let battle commence!

24.9.76
Our first hen's eggs from the chicks K has so carefully reared. The little white hen was in the henhouse practising her, 'I've laid an egg' cackle. The two remaining cocks were outside and crowing with pride and delight, both claiming, 'That's my wife, she's done it.'

The Island Council, 1977

back row, left to right, Lewis Glass, Basil Lavarello, Lars Repetto, Benny Green, Barton Green, Stanley Green, Terence Green; *front row, left to right*, Harold Green, Albert Glass, Administrator, Chaplain, Pamela Lavarello

The Island Council this afternoon was a long one, chiefly on account of the over-stocking of the limited pasture. They keep cattle and sheep by families and numbers are something of a status symbol. I was so bold as to suggest that they pool the lot and have one herd, one flock in which they all share. But I am only a new boy! I am much more sure about anti-litter!

I took Communion to old Emma this morning. Her granddaughter Joanna was walking away, but I asked her to stay; and presently little Iris walked in too. The Gospel reading had been from Matthew 18, about Jesus calling to him a little child. There were tears in Emma's eyes as I laid my hands in blessing on her old head. I think they were healing tears.

One of the crew of the *Tristania* came ashore to see the doctor about a damaged finger. A strange face seen suddenly on the island is a shock of surprise. And the *RSA* and *Hilary* also arriving has meant three mails in one week – surely a record!!

We now have several new arrivals, including two Australian scientists and Peter Inwood, a dentist from Harley Street. He is musical too and plays the organ.

25.9.76
Welcome sound and sight. The booming of a ship's fog horn announced a large ship passing close to our island. Later their radio officer had a long talk with our Administrator over the air, plying him with questions all about the island, in preparation for his broadcast on board his ship later on.

My anti-litter campaign is taking effect – small boys bring bits of broken glass, sometimes in the turn-ups of their pullovers.

18.10.76
I crave a holiday! Twelve months at a stretch and non-stop. A parson's ministry here may be on a small scale, but it is very concentrated and exposed and expectant! I could do with a break, and a bit of a change of scene. Where? When? How?

Three children of an expat family made their first appearance at the Children's Service. One of them afterwards took me for a walk, holding my hand. He looked up at me and said, "Father, you've got old hair." A delightfully candid comment on my ageing white and diminishing top-knot!

My temporary met. job has finished because a new expat has arrived to take over. I had some payment from South Africa for my work, and we put this money towards a new carpet ordered from Cape Town for this Chaplain's bungalow where we live. We will leave it here for future use.

25.10.76
As I was dressing I saw a distant mast above the horizon. Great excitement as presently this two-masted schooner approached. It was the *Wave Walker* with Gordon and Mary Cook on board and their two children and two more adults. They all came on shore and were very hospitably made welcome by the Administrator and his wife, and by the Chief Islander and Rose. We put on a buffet lunch, and very much enjoyed their company with new faces, and fresh topics of conversation.

Peter the dentist came to supper and for a game of chess. He offered to play an organ voluntary at the wedding next week, and I said I would ask our organist, Pamela Lavarello. When I did so, she told me I must never suggest anyone playing instead of her. Her husband was equally emphatic!

I have begun to prepare for Confirmation in two groups. The younger ones of 9-10 years old seem to be more keen and interested. Lily, who I thought too young for it, made quite sure she was going to be accepted for preparation.

Our little grey hen has started to lay again. K says she feels like praying, "Give us this day our daily egg."

The two scientist visitors, botanist and ecologist, Nigel Wace, and volcanist Cliff Olyer, are both waiting for favourable weather to get up to the peak.

11.11.76
Peter the dentist and Pat the sparker came to supper, and two boards out for chess afterwards.

I visited an old man and found him nursing a very painful swollen foot. The doctor had not been to see him for a couple of weeks. Shocking neglect and he has all the time in the world. I thought a prod from the padre would be timely.

21.11.76
Eddie and Rebecca Rogers' baby Tanya baptised this morning. Eddie is a Lay Reader along with Lars, and always very willing to help me in church.

3.12.76
There was a farewell party in the Prince Philip Hall for the Administrator and his wife going on leave. As usual beforehand I rather dread the dancing; but actually this time I quite enjoyed it. The variety and contrast among female partners can be quite entertaining. Dear Margaret, the Administrator's wife, so gentle and light as a feather, and we just drift along. Old Agnes, after dragging her up from her seat, gets settled in the tramlines, but

stays in reverse going backwards: no twisting and turning for her! And then there is Doris, a good dancer and she lets you know it. "I'm in charge of this one, because you can't dance, and I can." And although she is small, she is very strong. She grasps you firmly round the waist, and propels you round the floor under her control.

K suggested "How bright these glorious spirits shine" for an old islander's funeral today. I said, "No, I think he needs time for a bit of polishing before we could sing that hymn for him."

Funerals here are a great pastoral opportunity with a packed church, and full attendance. And then we all go to the cemetery so near by.

9.12.76
A very interesting lecture by Nigel Wace on this island's story, of which he has made such a careful study, together with colour slides. He showed us reproductions of Augustus Earle's paintings, which date from 1824.

And perhaps we should heed Nigel's solemn warnings. He had charts and figures to show how occupation of the island has steadily and progressively exploited its natural resources. The early settlers wrote into its constitution, that the means of livelihood and existence should be equally shared among all.

11.12.76
This island is hard to get to, and sometimes not easy to get away from it. The Administrator Stan Trees, and his wife Margaret, Peter the dentist and Cliff the volcanist, are all prepared with life-jackets, baggage, etc.; and the *Tristania* restless at her moorings.

Farewells and kisses; and all are ready to embark from the harbour. But low cloud and heavy rain and big swell... To be, or not to be??

St. Mary's Church

And there is Lindsay, our expert weatherman, gazing out to sea, and taking the whole situation into careful consideration... In due course he makes his decision – "No, not today."

Later Bill Sandham was sworn in as Magistrate and Acting Administrator. In the oath taken by Bill, Tristan da Cunha is described as "Colony of..." – one of the last bits of pink which used to be so numerous in the atlas of my early schooldays, and the British Empire?

Beverley was missing from the Confirmation class and I sent out a search party. They brought back the message, "You can tell Father that I'll come when I want to come; and not when I don't want to come."

13.12.76
Chief Willie Repetto died in hospital. Auntie Martha is very distressed over her beloved brother's passing. He had been Chief for a very long time, and when he retired in 1970 the title stuck... Another sadness for Martha Rogers has been that her beloved husband Arthur died while they were in England, and is buried in Fawley.

At his funeral I said that the best tribute and memorial to Chief Willie would be a real effort and determination to maintain all that is good and wholesome in the life of our island and community.

20.12.76
After the time it took in the harbour trussing up five calves, and getting them and all the tackle on board, I joined a 'meat' trip to Stoney Beach. When we got there the calves were released. The men got busy shooting adult cattle, and cutting them up, and then getting the pieces back into the cramped space on the boat.

I occupied myself visiting the penguin rookeries, noisy and smelly, but amusing too. I took photographs of the fine views of Nightingale and Inaccessible islands.

Before the end of the day a nice piece of fresh meat was brought round to our house by Brenda, and later little Sandra came with a gift of new potatoes. Aren't we lucky!

The *Hilary* brought a disabled yacht in tow. It had been drifting for a couple of days with its rudder gone, and its radio out of action, and with engine trouble too! Two South Africans and five Argentinians on board. Later they were away again, but very grateful for help and necessary repairs.

CHRISTMAS 1976
There were about one hundred and thirty at the midnight service; and they were all in church soon after 10 o'clock! I put on a seasonal filmstrip, as they all sat silently waiting.

The *Lindblad Explorer* could be seen out to sea as we got up, and presently it anchored nearby.

We had offered to give lunch to two of the passengers; and we much enjoyed the company of our lady guests. Among the passengers were Mr and Mrs Roger Peterson, who came to tea with us. I got him to autograph my copy of the bird book of which he is part author.

One of the happiest moments of this day was at our Children's Service in the morning. In the middle of it we were invaded by about two dozen of the ship's passengers complete with their equipment, photographic and for sound recording. A bit distracting, but also adding to the happiness of this festival celebration. A couple arrived just as we finished, and they were very distressed to have missed the service. I said to them, "Do come in and we'll have prayers together." And they did.

26.12.76

Tristan really shows off to the visitors! A fiercesome NE wind whipped up the sea into great white crested waves under drenching rain – and this in complete contrast to the lovely summer's day yesterday! The *Lindblad Explorer* had disappeared! We are told that some of the passengers were so entranced by our fascinating group of islands that they had asked the captain if the ship could dally for a day or two. Perhaps they had changed their minds?

A man said to me, "I hope that ship hasn't left any germs." They think it has happened in the past under similar circumstance, and that it could happen again.

We did not expect this fearful threatened attitude; but some deliberately shut themselves in their houses against such an invasion from the outside world!

We are hungry for letters and news. We have had no mail since October 13. It does make you feel cut-off and remote. And a very lonely island.

But mail will be taken soon on *Hilary*, so we must get busy with our writing. Mail must go out, as well as coming in.

Inaccessible Island, about twenty miles across the sea to the west.
Photograph from Michael Swales of the Denstone Expedition Trust.

Tethered – 1977 – To Tristan

5.1.77
Five girls keep the church clean and tidy on a weekly rota. We had them into our house for fun and games and light refreshments.

There is a penguin in a neighbour's hen run, and the hens seem to accept it. Perhaps it intends to stay there while it moults away its time.

13.1.77
Frank's funeral. He was a grand old man with his great big beard and venerable appearance. But ever young in heart and a great lover of children, especially his entrancing two year old granddaughter, Fiona.

With a gentle kindly disposition he was also so brave and patient and cheerful through the past weeks and months of his distressing illness. He had sincere faith, and I saw it in the look of serene composure as he lay back in his chair after receiving the sacrament last week in his home.

This evening there was a full room including his dear old widow, Clara. And such a relaxed atmosphere, not just sorrowful silence; but plenty of talk and laughter, which was good. May he rest in peace.

16.1.77
We are all on tenterhooks for the arrival of the mail on *Melodie*. We hear that there are twenty-two bags of it. They say she has left Cape Town. We gaze out to sea, but the ocean is very big and very empty! Impatient I went to the radio shack to get any news of the

ship. Yes, they had been in communication; but I was told, "She doesn't know where she is." Oh dear! Lost at sea?

21.1.77
Melodie has made it and is here – with the mail! And for us two-hundred and thirty items of it! But we had to wait fourteen weeks! And it included Christmas cards and calendars!

I went to see a boy, who had a nasty fall over the handlebars on his bike and damaged his face. It had left him with a painful thumb joint too. That was yesterday, and he had been taken to hospital and cleaned up. I was very surprised that the doctor had not been to see him today. On this island individual care is so possible, and lack of attention is inexcusable. I went to see the doctor.

A large package from the USA arrived addressed to the Chaplain. There were seven parcels inside addressed to specific families, which I took round to them. That was not at all right, and I got into trouble. "You done wrong, Father; and Mother very angry with you." "Oh," I said, "why?" "They parcels were all for our family," I was told. It left me puzzled and perplexed.

28.1.77
Eight long boats have left for Nightingale to get the first load of precious guano fertiliser.

The doctor seems to think he is in a busy practice in England, and should only be required to keep surgery hours for people to come to him; and only to be called out in cases of dire necessity. In this very small community he can and should be far more flexible and readily available.

Merlin continues to visit us, although her owners are back. She comes into our garden, and as soon as the door is opened she is inside, and lies down in my study. I had to put a rope round her neck and take her back. We are delighted to be remembered so fondly.

In church a young lady appeared to have no bra under a loose fitting blouse, and she was showing such shapely soft pink bosoms – intentional maybe? How Samuel Pepys would have enjoyed it. He sometimes in church did not object to this kind of distraction. His diary is my bedside book just now.

Wilting weather I call these damp humid days with cotton wool mist covering the base, and a warm muggy wind making me feel in a state of lethargy and collapse. And it brings out a flurry of tiny flies, which are all over our food.

Two or three of my servers in church have signed off. But Connie said to me, "Father, why have some of them given up serving?" I said I wasn't sure why, but some sort of grievance, I suppose. "But it's not you they are serving," he said, "it is the Lord." "You are absolutely right, Connie," I said, "I wish they could see it that way."

6.2.77
Queen's Jubilee. In the evening epilogue on the radio I spoke on thinking back to 1952 and the very demanding challenge to Princess Elizabeth, young wife and mother, remembering her courage, dedication and resolve. We thought of her sense of duty and responsibility, her family life with Prince Philip, and thanked God for her Christian faith and good example. Later there was a program of fun and games, and a dance in the evening.

Our two pullets produced their first egg. We are thinking of calling them 'Silver' and 'Jubilee'.

We heard that a passenger liner would be passing and would call for any mail we had ready. We got busy writing for posting. The big Holland/America liner appeared on time. But, alas, it was too rough for our launch to put out to sea; so the liner proceeded on its way to Cape Town without our letters. Rather different from a pillarbox round the corner at home!

There's a lot of sickness about and has been for some time. They attribute it to the germs brought onto the island by visitors off the ship at Christmas. They call it 'ship sickness.'

17.2.77
Fishing day, and the first since November 18. Nearly three months is an unusually long gap.

After church on Sunday we usually visit someone, and this time it was to a couple to congratulate them on the arrival of a grandson. He was in church this morning with his parents, just ten days old!

21.2.77
We had the chance of a trip on the old barge to Sandy Point. This gave us an opportunity to wander and enjoy the setting of trees, of which there are none at the settlement.

Three ducks have arrived on the island, exciting visitors and surely welcome. Some of us hoped they would stay, and give us a chance for close study and identification. But they were met by a man with a gun. I wrote a note of protest to the Administrator.

23.2.77
Ash Wednesday 7 a.m. Holy Communion, 9 a.m. School service, 10 a.m. Litany and prayers, 3 p.m. Confirmation class, 6 p.m. Evensong, 10 p.m. Radio epilogue. Retired priest fully occupied!

Mail dependent upon shipping is very much a feature of life here, with the inevitable fluctuations and uncertainties. Deprivation; then hope, expectation, anticipation, realisation, appropriation, appreciation, just about spells it out. And with the ship and the mail come bulk delivery of newspapers, etc. for expats to share around, and to pore over for several days.

A large Italian tanker, *Emma Prima*, came in close and anchored. The captain and some of the crew came ashore. Later several of us expats went out on the factory barge, and we were invited on board the tanker. From the bridge it was possible to get a vivid impression of the enormous length of this 130,000 ton vessel; and even more so when I was allowed to walk and pace the deck. The captain was dressed quite informally in slacks and a pullover, and he spoke fluent English, and so did the third mate, a woman, whose husband was second mate.

The tanker was on its way to Rio de Janeiro. I had an idea! Couldn't it take us on board, and later drop us off on its way back? Just for a blissful break!? South America and back. Tantalising day dream!

25.3.77
Lady Day and on this island with its church dedication to the Blessed Virgin Mary, the parish priest is accused of deception and theft! I never thought it would come to this. It was that parcel from the USA, and suspicion following.

In this small community it can poison relationships. An impossible situation and most unpleasant. I asked the Acting Administrator to arrange a public meeting. This he did; and he conducted the enquiry fairly and openly, patiently defusing the bomb. Some of those present were outspoken in their comments and accusations. One old man was even threatening. I couldn't help recollecting a question put to me by a lady shortly before we left England, "How do you think the natives will treat you?" At that time I smiled to reassure her.

When the meeting was over K, anxious for reconciliation, the same evening took a birthday present around to Gillian of the offended household, and she was welcomed. Olive said with reference to all the fuss, "It's all over, and finished now." Peace restored, and confidence, I hope. Now I am mighty glad to be rid of this unhappy episode. And all so unnecessary. And clean contrary to the friendly nature of most of them.

28.3.77
A perfect day of blue sky and warm sun and a gentle breeze. We took out a picnic lunch and scrambled up Hillpiece. Even in this confined space it is possible to get away; or anyhow to feel like it.

A large moth was caught in one of the houses. It had a five-inch wingspan and brown and green under its wings. Although rather damaged, there were signs of distinctive marking on the top of its large body. Is it a native: if not, how did it get here?

7.4.77
Good Friday and a packed church by 12 noon. Some had arrived at 10.30 and sat silently waiting. And many stayed for the Three Hours service.

EASTER 1977
We had services at 7 and 8.30 am and many communicants.
My theme this Eastertide has been Jesus risen and alive, oh yes; but also out and about. And not shut up in church, nor confined to his sacrament. A message needed, I think, to link faith and everyday life. And there was a full church at the Children's

Service at 10.30 including Matthew Green's baptism, with celebrations following in his home.

We saw a bird rather like a moorhen running along our garden wall. We learned that it was a purple gallinule; and they do occasionally visit here. A nice afternoon and we were up the hillside and a starchy (Tristan thrush) came to see what we were doing.

27.4.77

Winter has hit us suddenly. One day basking in the sun on our 'p and q patch' (peace and quiet) on the other side of the lava; and the next day it's long pants and pullover.

A syrup tin had got stuck firmly onto a donkey's front foot. It was quite willing for me to lift that leg and pull off the offending object. And grateful too, I think.

Harold in to tell me he could not be Churchwarden along with a woman. Oh dear! I did wonder whether we had been moving too fast. Even with bringing women on to the Parish Church Council was apparently rather a new idea.

6.5.77
Island Council chaired by the Acting Administrator. It was interesting and useful; and we touched on many matters – pension schemes, long boats, films and showings, cemetery, feral cats, ratting, sheep and cattle, island stores. At the end there was expressed thanks to Bill for all his good work as Acting Administrator, and good wishes to him and his family for their future.

13.5.77
Tristania came in to anchor at first light, bringing back the Administrator and his wife, and also a new teacher for the school, Christine Stone; and for us nearly one-hundred and fifty letters and seventeen parcels. Whoopee!!

A new doctor has come, and the present doctor and his wife are departing. They are taking with them one of our most promising young people, which is such a pity.

The ship's departure was delayed by a terrific storm. Huge waves came right in and over the harbour wall, washing off three factory power boats and a lot of tackle. It was all hands to the harbour to rescue the remaining boats, and drag them to safety on higher ground.

A purple gallinule is frequenting our patch. With some hen food we are encouraging it to stay.

29.5.77

An important arrival on the island is the new addition to the teaching staff of the school. Christine Stone is a very lively person in body, mind, yes, and spirit. She is eager to share our church life, and has already started an 11-plus youth group. Teenagers have responded eagerly and on one wet evening she had twenty in her house! And this at a time when I had been feeling at rather a low ebb in my work here. How thankful we are!

I rather think that something else that has attracted her is that there is a sizeable mountain upon which she can exercise and test her climbing experience and skill. She is unhappy and restless about the restrictions on her movements.

K with foresight brought out some canvas and wool, and I am finding rug making a pleasant occupation and diversion. Sometimes we expats miss the more fully-occupied life of the islanders with their fishing, cattle, sheep, patches and potatoes, regular expeditions to Sandy Point, Stoney Beach, caves; and of course Nightingale, with their shacks and huts.

1.6.77

Ratting Day

We took Christine with her dog out on the patches, but as last year not a rat to be seen. Spasmodic activity around the walls by men with their dogs and their trapping devices.

11.6.77

St. Barnabas. Such a lovely dawn as we walked up to the church, with a pale turquoise sky and grey clouds tinged with roseate hues; and this in stark contrast to the hard outline of the grim grey lava.

Later we took out a picnic lunch and basked in the warm

sunshine. Pansies and primroses were out, and butterflies. And this is mid-winter!

The new doctor (who has been here before) is settling in well. He knows what he's here for and how to do it. He is constantly out and about, and regular in visiting where and when it may be opportune.

Rita and Valerie came and asked for help in making a dress for Vanessa's birthday, aged 2. Mrs Buxton is now addressed as 'K', and Val told her, "K, you have got better in playing the piano and organ. You weren't very good when you first came, but you've got better." And looking at a photo of our daughter Mary, she said, "If she was on the island, all the boys would love her, and so would the children."

'Shib', the doctor, says he has heard islanders' criticism of my mention of the alcohol problem here. I take note, but I think my ministry will always link religion and life.

To the shore with K to uplift loads of kelp and rotting fish to manure our kitchen garden.

21.6.77
And the shortest day! Now we can look forward to longer daylight and spring and summer.

The Island Council has been informed that there is available a grant from the Queen's Jubilee Appeal Fund and there is the question how best to use it. The Administrator suggested improvements to the pub to make it more attractive. I disagreed when we know it is suggested that it could be used for "community youth projects". Let it be used rather for improvements to the Prince Philip Hall and its general use.

24.6.77
A very pleasant evening at the Residency, when Stan and Margaret Trees welcomed just sixteen expats. It was rather nice to be relaxed as just ourselves!

20.7.77
A Church Council meeting in our house and a good one, and lively with full agenda. There was the question about some funds from church boxes in Lent and Advent. I told them about Christian Aid and its work. They remembered the 1961 volcano disaster to the island and help they received, and they agreed to send a donation.

14.8.77
Anniversary Day. This is to commemorate William Glass coming to the island in 1816; and later he decided to settle here. There was a cricket match at which I was umpire. In the evening a reception was followed by a dance in the hall.

28.8.77
Tristania came with thirty-three bags of mail on board after fifteen weeks letterless. We scored one hundred and sixty letters and twenty-five packages. The ship also brought a new 'sparker' (post and radio) with his wife and their three children.

At night there was a fluttering and knocking against the window by a bird attracted by the light, and I caught it. We were told it was a white-faced storm petrel by our ornithologist, who took a photograph of it before I let it go.

The Administrator has called for a restriction on the number of penguin eggs being taken.

I have written to him on behalf of Christine Stone to set her free to mountaineer!

15/9/77
Dear Stan,
I am writing on behalf of Christine Stone, hoping that you may have given this matter further thought. Her past life and experience, I think, does justify special consideration and treatment.

She is quite exceptional as an expat coming from Scotland with its mountains, and her work and responsibilities there with young people outdoors, as well as her wider experiences elsewhere.

I reckon that with her mountaineering and climbing experience she could knock spots off most, if not all, the islanders; and I am sure she is careful and sensible. It must be very frustrating for her to be denied freedom to roam, and to be confined to this small area.

Do put yourself in her shoes – and set her free!

Summer is coming and longer days and better weather; and for Christine the urge to range wider. Please let her go. She does not know that I am writing or approaching you again on her behalf. – this is just a private note between me and you.

I do know that it would give her great encouragement in all her life and work here, if you set her free.

Truly yours,
Edmund

5.9.77

Two years to the day since I sailed from Southampton on the Union Castle boat the *Pendennis Castle* for Cape Town.

Christine Stone has been tackling 'sex' in an open discussion with her 11-plus young people, wisely and sensibly and helpfully, I'm sure.

19.10.77

Bishop Leslie Stradling came on the *RSA*. He stays with us and he is a charming and delightful guest. He is kept fully occupied with church and school and visiting homes. He takes a lively and personal interest in the life of the place with his camera and recording cassette.

The way he took the Confirmation service was very special, making it a significant occasion and memorable for the young candidates.

Bishop Leslie Stradling and Tristan children

But 'ship sickness' with coughs and colds and sneezes all around the community, and they blame the *RSA* for causing it.

3.11.77

Fourteen at Communion this morning for All Souls. I had asked for names to read out for remembrance. Old Agnes gave me a list, almost unintelligible and astonishing spelling! I asked her to interpret ... "Father, can't you read?" she rebuked me.

7.11.77

A wild wind all day went on noisily into the night. I was so restless that I got up and dipped into my Barsetshire novel with Trollope's vivid description of Mr Harding in his old age. K got out of bed to see what had become of me, and she coaxed me back with a nice cup of Ovaltine. Peggy is very kindly supplying us with milk from her cow, and at no charge.

Christine is set free! After signing a solemn document drawn up by the Administrator, she accepts full responsibility for herself in case of any accident or mishap. She signs very willingly, and leaps for joy! So one of my campaigns is successful, but the same could not be said with reference to litter, conservation and alcohol.

I have been growing a beard, and I am surprised and amused when I see my face in the mirror, and find it hard to believe that it belongs to me.

Albatross

17.11.77

A knock at the door at 6 a.m. and Stanley Swain says it is today for the base. A lovely morning, but cloud never lifted off the peak. We climbed up the side of a gulch which was hard going, and we were thankful for occasional pauses. Up on the base we wandered about in the bog fern for a couple of hours. Stan took hold of a nesting mollie (albatross) and contrived to show us its great wing span, as I took a photo of it.

We had splendid views of Nightingale and Inaccessible. Coming back we skidded down the red sand, and then the long trudge home. I reckon we must have walked about eight miles to the Bluff and back, plus two more miles and a stiff climb to the top of the base. Ready for bath and bed.

24.11.77

At last! There were two factory launches going to Nightingale with materials for the shacks there, and they offered to take us. It was rather rough, and we arrived cold and wet from sea spray. We soon dried off, walking around the line of small dwellings; and then seeing something of the wildlife on Nightingale. There were mollies (albatross) on their nests, and lots of starchies (thrushes) and buntings (they call them canaries).

We left the island with a great many petrels which for their fat the men had pulled out of their holes and killed – a grim and sad sight after so much to delight the eye. Often on a Tristan expedition there is shedding of blood.

On our way back across the sea the Tristan mountain looked so impressive with its snow white peak above a collar of cloud. It took four hours each way.

We have had one hundred copies of the Good News Bible from

USPG*. This gives us the opportunity of presenting a Bible to each household.

Alfred Rogers and Rhoda Lavarello were married – a happy service followed by a reception in the hall, with plenty to eat and drink.

One day a silver sea reflecting dazzling light. The next day a gale whipping the sea into crested racing waves, the wind-driven spray outpacing them.

> *To the Administrator, Tristan da Cunha. 16 January 1978*
> *LITTER*
> *I must report a really shocking case of litter: a horrid dump of cans, bottles (including broken glass), vegetable matter, etc. has been left at the bottom of the waterfall just across the lava to the east. This is all the more a shame because it is one of the fair and pleasant spots within easy reach of the settlement.*
> *It was brought to my notice and I have been to investigate. It is most unpleasantly a fact.*
> *Edmund*

4.12.77

Second Sunday in Advent and Bible Sunday

We were able thankfully to acknowledge the recent gift of one hundred Good News Bibles, and to dedicate the larger specially bound copy for use in the church on the lectern.

7.12.77

An Investiture. Albert Glass, Chief Islander and Police Sergeant has been awarded the British Empire Medal, and it was pinned on his chest by the Administrator. This took place in the Council Chamber full of islanders and expats, with refreshments following.

---

* *United Society for the Propagation of the Gospel, and the Society which appointed me as Chaplain here.*

Last – 1978 – Lap

12.1.78
I was asked to bless two new homes by their request, Alfred and Rhoda.

Jimmy offered to clean up and repaint the woodwork behind the altar in church. I readily agreed and welcomed his initiative. He is making a good job of it, with Felicity to help him.

Christine has achieved her ambition and climbed the mountain peak. Later on she and another expat, Neil, walked right round the island in two days.

We were taken out in the factory launch all round the island, a good way to encompass and comprehend this mountain in the sea together with clear views of its peak. We stopped to fish and struck a shoal of blue fish. I caught three all at once on three hooks on my line, and K caught a whopper of about 40 pounds.

I am getting around the houses with a gift of the Good News Bible, always assured of a welcome with a present in hand.

Expats Ben and Maggie Claxton suggested a fancy dress party, each of us choosing a Shakespeare or a Dickens character. K went as Betsy Trotwood from David Copperfield, and I as a gravedigger in Hamlet, which suited me down to the ground.

19.1.78
Mail on *Melodie*. Over one hundred and fifty items in our bag, and such fulsome variety of correspondents including: Diana Reader Harris, Keith Richmond, Eric Kingsnorth, Hugh

Alexander, Ian Mackintosh, George Shrimpton, David Gomall SJ, Tony Maunsell, Leslie Stradling (Bishop), Jena Dunkerley, Godfrey Buxton, Ciceley Smethwick, Ros Mills, etc., etc.

What a feast for human castaways! Representing all sorts of relationships and fascinating links at different times with people and places. Oh, and one from Sara Kumiko in Japan; and *three* from Lady Rosamond Fisher (Archbishop's widow) addressed to The Reverend Canon E. Buxton, 'Come wind, come weather', Tristan da Cunha. We had used John Bunyan's words as a title of some of our circular letters.

We saw some flying fish, really exciting and quite spectacular with their large transparent 'wings', or are they fins? They jump out of the water, then do long hovering flight of about a hundred yards before dipping back into the sea again.

8.2.78
Ash Wednesday and a school service in church. Give me a congregation of lively children under control and behaving, a captive audience; and I'm well away. I can let myself go and hold their attention and elicit their response. Good for me, and I hope for them too!

Old Gertie said, "Whatever will that priest do next?" because I got some girls to dance down the aisle singing, 'Jesus' love is very wonderful.' Dancing in church – in Lent! Tut, tut!

10.2.78
Queen's Day and lovely weather. I was asked to play in the cricket match. As I walked out to bat Lindsay called out, "Don't forget, boys, it's Lent. No catches in Lent, the padre's coming in."

Mail came on *Hilary*. About fifty items for us, including ten calendars for 1978. So great a variety of pictures in the post!

Seven boats away to Nightingale reduces Sunday church attendance. At the Children's Service K had thoughtfully marshalled the babies, so that baby Matthew could not pull the hair of the girl in front of him, as he had done on the previous Sunday.

19.2.78
A ship passed and lowered a raft with gifts for the island – timber, books, magazines, toys, etc. This was left on the shore late in the evening. By next morning canisters had been broken into and all was stolen. Shameful and shocking behaviour!

Christine Stone took half a dozen older girls up to the base, preparing for their Duke of Edinburgh awards.

1.3.78
And 70 years from 1908. And when it became known, we had many kind callers and gifts. I have scored thirteen pairs of locally knitted socks. At the end of the day on my radio epilogue I was able to thank everybody for such a happy and memorable birthday.

I told them that my one big disappointment was that I had not been able to celebrate the special date by climbing right to the top of the peak. I am sure Christine Stone would willingly have been my guide with a helping hand.

5.3.78
This afternoon two young boys, Robin and Darren, brought along a stone to show me; but it was really by way of an entrance ticket to refreshment and games and talk. Yes, talk. When Darren gets going he is non-stop. We can only catch perhaps one or two words in a dozen. His face is all that matters, and I am happy just

to watch that; and only to make a few responsive noises myself.

We have been having some beautiful sunrises and sunsets. This evening the sky was pastel shades of grey with turquoise and cerise patches above the sea.

We had a long walk to Runaway Beach, and then a dip in a rock pool. I felt seventy years young.

14.3.78
An international incident added a bit of variety to Tristan life. A Taiwan fishing vessel was caught trespassing in our water. It was escorted back here for proceedings to be taken.

The captain could not speak a word of English, and their radio officer only very little; so communication was difficult. They have been made captive in our nice comfortable guest cabin, with kind and gentle Margaret Swain to look after them. Their fishing tackle and catch have been confiscated and a fine imposed.

We discovered that the radio officer is a Christian, and I took him to show him the church. I tried to discover what church he might belong to. We got rather lost in suggesting possibilities. He cut short my inquisitive enquiries with a satisfying and sufficient answer – "Only Jesus." Enough said.

I visited Auntie Martha who I heard had not been well. There she sat as usual in the corner of her room, and with two young visitors who had come to see 'Auntie', as they all call her. What a delightful feature of island life is this constant interspersed visiting – a sort of drawing the community together with laces of love.

On Good Friday during the Three Hours I had three meditations under headings – the volcano, the rainbow, the cross.

Spinning wheel

3.4.78

Lindsay and Gladys Lavarello are very kindly making possible our one real holiday in our three years here. They have invited us to join them in their shack on Stoney Beach on the opposite side of the island. Accommodation is not much more than a shed with no windows, just a door. They brought with them their seven year old grandson Martin, and the five of us pretty well filled the floor space, which was covered with dry grass. We slept side by side in a row, like sardines in a tin.

There were no toilet facilities, just a matter of disappearing out of sight; and a dip in the sea for a bathe bath. There was fresh water in a small spring nearby. The weather was kind with lovely bright days, apart from a chilly wind at times.

Our kind host and hostess had brought some provisions, including potatoes for sure; and we fished off the rocks. And our meals included meat, berry pie, Tristan pudding, and nice porridge to start the day on a cold morning.

We enjoyed watching rockhopper penguins, as they watched us. We walked along the shore to Cave Point, one of the most beautiful parts of the island. Martin found a small octopus in a pool which cut up into useful bait for our fishing. We saw, I think, about a hundred seals in Seal Bay.

And after a week what a welcome back to the Edinburgh settlement and home. Little Pam at the harbour with a thermos for tea, and later she brought round a cooked lunch. So thoughtful and kind.

It had been for us a most original, enjoyable and exceptional holiday. A memory for a lifetime!

9.4.78
We kept Harvest Festival and St Mary's Church was looking so colourful with flowers and vegetables. I told them that a most important 'patch' is here in this church, and God is looking for a harvest of good behaviour in our lives, and outside the church.

There is a strong sense of pride and complacency. "We're different on Tristan." "We know best." "You can't tell us or teach us." But then it is their small homemade dominion.

16.4.78
With Christine we tackled another way up the base, rather more difficult and a stiffer climb. It included a nasty spot at crossing on a loose surface over a very steep drop. I lost my foothold and I was very thankful for the grip of a strong helping hand. We got to the ponds up the Lagoon gulch with running water. And we had

splendid views of the peak.

Boom! Boom! Boom! in the middle of the night woke us up. We looked out to see the lights of a passing ship. I hoped Tristan would have had an answering signal.

This is exam week in the school. I set some questions for my Scripture class. One of them, asked to write out the Lord's Prayer, put it as, 'Our Father, who art in heaven, hollow be thy name...' In telling the story of the Good Samaritan in their own words, one wrote about 'a dangerous road to Jericho were robbers lark behind huge bulldozers.'

In the Children's Service I talked about kindness to animals, after having seen boys throwing stones at penguins and seals.

19.4.78
Big kerfuffle in the harbour this morning with the possibility of Nightingale – men carrying equipment, women carrying provisions, trailers loaded with stores. To go, or not to go?? The weather looked unsettled and the sea a bit rough... then a radio message from *Hilary* fishing off Nightingale that the sea swell was bad around there. And it was off!!

A little egret paid us a visit just outside our gate. It is such a lovely bird white with yellow beak and thin dark grey legs.

Winter has suddenly arrived after a long lingering period of welcome warmth. The wind from the south brings a sharp nip from the antarctic snow and ice!

Jean told me that her Stanley is thrilled with their copy of the Good News Bible. "He was always reading thrillers; but now it's this Bible, and he can't put it down."

We so often have wonderful skies at sunrise and sunset. This morning as I dressed I watched a great dark grey cloud over the sea catch alight, and presently the whole glowed as if it was incandescent. And this exciting transformation was reflected in the seawater below.

2.5.78

Tristania here with mail, and about one hundred and twenty items for us, including a big package from the USA with gifts inside. I made sure this time of no mistake or misunderstanding in the opening and distribution!

The ship had to retreat to the lee of the island owing to high winds and very rough sea. Last night there was a storm about the mountain with thunder and lightning and torrents of rain making waterfalls.

There had been some discussion about my successor as chaplain here. This time there is the possibility of an appointment from South Africa, where the situation in connection with apartheid is very tense. The Administrator and the Fishing Factory Director from Cape Town are very concerned that the next Chaplain here must be a white man. They were sure that anybody less than white would 'empty the church.' Oh dear! contagion from South Africa!

I took Communion to Emma, old and frail, but so devout and responsive in her own quiet way. And also in the room were young mother Margaret and her babe, for her Thanksgiving after childbirth. Worship can include all ages, and occasions.

A gallinule in our garden was a joyful surprise.

Christine Stone has been up to the peak again. This is in accordance with her self-imposed schedule and program of the

peak once each month! So this is the fifth time this year for her*
who at first was strictly forbidden even to attempt it!

Ken came in this evening to play chess in the first round of the
island chess competition. I won, and he asked for a second game,
which I also won.

In the storm last week three roofs were blown off.

14.5.78
Whitsunday. And it's not difficult in this part of the world to talk
about the 'wind' of the Holy Spirit at Pentecost!

We have made a list of houses we would like to visit again
before we go, and today it was to Joan and Bernard. Also in the
room was Darren's lovely face and curly hair, and his little
enchantress of a sisters, Marie. And for good measurement add
another generation, old Grandma Gertie – vintage Tristan!

13.6.78
Mothers Union brought thirty women to a service in the church.
Afterwards we all went to the Residency, where Margaret Trees
kindly had us all to tea. The women, as is their wont, all sat
around the room in total silence – until the games. And when it
came to throwing playing cards into a bucket, there were fits of
laughter – especially when one tried to cheat by moving nearer to
the bucket. I was directing that game, so I seized Monica by her
hair and pulled her back to where she ought to be. The padre's
prompt action caused much merriment round the room. I can hear
them laughing still!

* *After leaving Tristan Christine Stone took up work with the United Mission in Nepal – mountainous enough for her? For more than twenty years she has done a great work there for education in the schools together with her Christian faith and witness. She has been awarded an OBE.*

We were told that there is a female elephant seal on Hottentot beach, and we went to see it. I took some photographs of the huge creature.

The chess competition goes on. I had a good game with Cyril. He threatened me early on, and I had to concentrate hard to extricate myself, and finally "I won him", as they say.

A deep sound from the sea awoke me. I jumped out of bed and I saw a passing ship all lit up. Those on board must have had a striking view of this island mountain under a brilliant full moon.

27.6.78
Psalm 19 in school prayers this morning. C S Lewis calls it "The greatest poem in the Psalter, and one of the greatest lyrics in the world." It is so comprehensive, dealing with God and nature, God and morality, matter and spirit. I tried to tell the children to keep their eyes open; and also to watch their behaviour, by way of trying to explain it.

The factory put on a dance this evening to celebrate a thousand cases of fish sent for export.

1.7.78
I saw a cat for the first time on Tristan, when I climbed to the top of the new volcano. I wanted to get a photo of it 'smocking' as the islanders speak of it. Cats now are feral, having gone wild from previous domestic cats. This one was a dark tabby.

The cattle egrets have disappeared. Where to? and how? They with their slow wing beats look so frail to face flight across the ocean.

Christine up the peak for the sixth time this year, keeping up her monthly aloft schedule!

8.7.78

The 'dong' sounded early for a fishing day, but can they be sure so early and so dark? The barometer falling steadily warned the fishermen assembling at the harbour. They decided not to venture and rightly so, as it turned out a very wet and windy day with a rough sea.

Stan and Margaret Trees gave a party for the seven girls who have won the Duke of Edinburgh award, and thanked their helpers.

A home Communion service for Clara in her bed. Her daughter Peggy asked to come too, and said that Ernest is in the kitchen, could he join us? Of course! And for good measure little Fiona came in and sat on Peggy's lap in a nice blue dress with bright red stockings. Communion congregational and colourful.

17.7.78

K was up in the hospital sharing in the night watch on Mabel. The next night I was at her bedside all night, until she died. After the funeral Stephen took my hand, and said, "Thank you and Katharine for all you did for my Mother."

20.7.78

Vanessa's third birthday, and we joined in the celebration. Judy and Ken have been enlarging their house, but it is not finished yet. A big empty space is well used by twenty or more women carding or spinning. Fifteen spinning wheels in action. Talk about home industries!

24 .7.78
I had to get past two spinning wheels to visit a boy in his bed, and there I found the doctor also on a visit. So doctor and parson on a combined visitation in one small bedroom; and mother Beatrice kindly brought us cups of tea, as we sat on the bed.

30.7.78
Our wedding anniversary. We thought we'd have a festive celebration at home and asked four friends to lunch, Gertie Lavarello, Clara Glass, Maud Swain and Agnes Swain. We didn't tell them it was a special date until they arrived. A happy party and domestic celebration!

7.8.78
At our last Church Council Meeting I wanted to help to prepare them for the period until another padre would be coming to take my place, but Lars made it clear that he would be in charge. They were quite keen on my suggestion of a great cross set up in the open on Clay Point – a sure sign to passing ships that this is an island with a resident Christian community.

1.9.78
At the last meeting of the Island Council Albert Glass, the Chief Islander, paid tribute to the departing Administrator, "Stan has been a decent bloke," he said.

After a night of furious wind and rain a very cold raw damp morning with snow on top o the base and waterfalls down it.

9.9.78
Mail on *Melodie*. It is eighteen weeks since the last mail on May 5 and on the text on our calendar this morning was, "He satisfieth the longing soul." Yes, and there were one hundred and twenty items in our mail bag.

A new Administrator, Eddie Brooks, and his wife Jennie have arrived; and also a new schoolmaster and his wife and their three children.

We had a great scramble and climb with Christine as companion and guide and helping hand. We went up Hottentot gulch to the top of the base, and then on nearly to Nellie's Hump, and I suppose to about 4,000ft. We had dreams of the peak, but it was too far on and that much higher. So that was our last climb and I admit defeat as far as the peak.

17.9.78
Sunday, and we were able to have our last service and Holy Communion in St. Mary's Church here this morning, which was so good.

The Sanctuary in St. Mary's Church

Later a long line of islanders beside the harbour road for formal and fond farewells; but not emotional. They are shy rather than demonstrative in public on such occasions. Male a handshake, female a kiss... We got into the barge and we were taken out of the harbour, and to get on board the *Tristania*.

Up anchor, and soon that mountain in the sea was no more than a distant speck across the ocean.

Soon after we came back the Tristan da Cunha Association was formed in England; and it makes a very useful link between the island and the wider world.

The Association has a strong membership, issues a half-yearly Newsletter, and holds a lively Annual General Meeting.

The President is Mr. Allan Crawford, FRGS
and the Secretary is:
>	Mr. M. K. Swales, FRGS
>	c/o Denstone College,
>	Uttoxeter
>	Staffordshire ST14 5HN
>	U.K.

Tristan Prayers

St. Mary's School

God our loving Father,
thank you for life and health
and this new day

Thank you for eyes to see
and ears to hear
a mind to think
and a mouth to speak

Thank you for lessons to learn
and games to play
for friendship and fun

Bless us this day
at school and at home

Bless our island and people
and their life and work
by land and sea

May we grow up
in body, mind and spirit
to be faithful followers
and eager disciples

of Jesus Christ
our Lord and Master. Amen.

Our Patron Saint, the Blessed Virgin Mary

Dear God,

As Mary said Yes to the angel
and was obedient to your will;
may we always be ready to do
what you want us to do,
        Like Mary

As Mary went to Elizabeth
to share their joy together;
may we bring happiness
wherever we go,
        Like Mary

Mary gave birth to her Son in a stable
and laid him in a manger,
because there was no room for them at the inn:
make us brave and sensible under difficulties,
        Like Mary

We think of Mary finding Jesus in the Temple,
and with him at the wedding in Cana;
may we be prepared for the unexpected
as we follow Jesus,
        Like Mary

May we draw near to the foot of the cross,
and discover its meaning,
        Like Mary

Keep us faithful in prayer and in fellowship,
and expecting the working of the Holy Spirit
in the Church,
        Like Mary

Children's Church
a prayer based on Luke 2.41 -52

LORD JESUS,
give me an eager enquiring mind,
asking questions,
and listening to answers,
      Like You

Lord Jesus,
give me a spirit of adventure
and the joy of discovery,
      Like You

Lord Jesus,
give me a love of the Church
that I may always be happy in God's house
and intent upon worship,
      Like You

Lord Jesus,
may I grow up in body, mind
and spirit,
      Like You